POSTERS

OF WORLD WAR II

POSTERS
OF WORLD WAR II

Compiled and Edited by G. H. Gregory

GRAMERCY BOOKS
New York ★ Avenel

*The editor and publisher wish to thank
the staff of the National Archives in Washington, D.C.,
for their help in the preparation of this book.
All photographs courtesy of National Archives.*

This 1993 edition is published by Gramercy Books,
distributed by Outlet Book Company, Inc.,
a Random House Company,
40 Engelhard Avenue,
Avenel, New Jersey 07001.

Random House
New York • Toronto • London • Sydney • Auckland

Book design by Kathryn Wolgast

Printed and bound in the United States of America

Library of Congress Cataloging-in-Publication Data
Posters of World War II.
p. cm.
ISBN 0-517-09318-9
1. World War, 1939-1945—Posters.   I. Gramercy Books (Firm)
II. Title: Posters of World War Two.
D743.25.P67   1993
940.53'022'2—dc20   93-27447
CIP

8 7 6 5 4 3 2 1

INTRODUCTION

THE POSTERS produced by various agencies of the United States and other governments during the two world wars were instruments of propaganda. The often negative connotation associated with propaganda derives especially from its use during peacetime by totalitarian regimes. In wartime, however, the use of bold graphic images and hard-hitting slogans to support a nation's struggle does not seem sinister—although it is no less manipulative—and poster propaganda is accepted as an appropriate weapon in the war effort. Apart from their function as purveyors of patriotism, wartime posters can also be masterful art—beautiful, affecting, and visually important works that combine pictures and words in original ways.

The significant use of the poster by the nations involved in World War I derived from the explosion in graphic design of the art nouveau period of the preceding two decades, as well as from a new facility in color printing. Italy, France, Germany, Russia, Hungary, and the United States were the major countries that produced a great deal of visual propaganda. These color images, with their immediate appeal and emotional messages, were their era's equivalent of today's mass-consumed television commercials.

During World War I many well-known artists were commissioned to create posters. The two shown here, issued in 1917, were used to raise money for the American Committee for Relief in the Near East. The moving illustration on the right was done by Ethel Franklin Betts Bain. The dramatic image far right was painted by Gordon Grant.

In 1918, the U.S. Treasury commissioned Charles Livingston Bull, a famous wildlife illustrator, to create this poster for the War Savings Stamps and Liberty Loans program. Bull lived near the New York Bronx Zoo and used many of its inhabitants as models. He was particularly concerned with the plight of the American eagle, which he used on at least two World War II posters.

KEEP HIM FREE

BUY

W.S.S.
WAR SAVINGS STAMPS
ISSUED BY THE
UNITED STATES
GOVERNMENT

WAR SAVINGS STAMPS

ISSUED BY THE UNITED STATES TREASURY DEPT.

KETTERLINUS, PHILA

The posters of World War I were, in style and substance, outgrowths of a nineteenth-century mentality, and were therefore serious, noble, sentimental, and symbolic; their images ranged from scenes in a realistic style to expressionist and art nouveau compositions. By World War II, most of the pretentious nobility and near-literary qualities in national posters were replaced by bolder and simpler images. Through succinct slogans they demanded involvement on the home front and featured more satire and humor as well as blatant mockery of the enemy.

An advertising-directed and consumer-oriented atmosphere had already become pervasive in the United States at the time of its entry into World War I in 1917. The nation's wartime posters are rather beautiful examples that supported the war effort with appeals to sacrifice. In some ways unlike the European posters of the period—perhaps because of the country's geographical distance from the conflict—U.S. posters were less stylistically daring, less angry and horror-evoking. They appealed to patriotism; they asked for support of the American Red Cross; they advertised government bonds and war savings stamps; and they promoted recruitment. Their images were realistic yet symbolic, serious and patriotic, even reserved. Among the artists were the best American illustrators of the period: Howard Chandler Christy, James Daugherty, Charles Livingston Bull, Edward Penfield, Gordon Grant—and, of course, James Montgomery Flagg, whose famed image of Uncle Sam pointing to the viewer and declaring "I Want You" was used for army recruitment in both world wars.

Like their European counterparts during World War II, what American posters lost in seriousness and high moral tone they gained in directness of expression, graphic and mass-appealing images, clever slogans, and satire and humor. The subjects of U.S. posters touched on every aspect of American wartime life—from enlistment in the armed forces to the recycling and conservation of resources in the home. The artistic styles reflected a consumer society grown sophisticated in the techniques of advertising.

These simple and immediately accessible images utilized slick realism as a predominant means of expression; many of them were designed around photographs, reflecting the influence of such popular photojournalist publications as *LIFE* and a background of regional documentary photography sponsored by the WPA and other agencies in the 1930s. The "This Is America: For This We Fight" series, for example, featured photographs of national monuments, and the "Produce for Victory" series incorporated photographs of ordinary Americans. The influence of magazine advertising and cover illustration is found in the pop-realism styles of many other posters—the "Enlist in the Army" posters for the Signal Corps, Engineers, and other units may be considered stylistic cousins of Coca-Cola ads.

The effort to bring all segments of society together in the common fight was reflected consistently in the posters, which showed men and women serving in the armed forces and working together on the home front to help in the war effort. Management and labor were asked to cooperate in "Together We Win," where a worker and a businessman shake hands, covered by the hand of Uncle Sam. Average citizens were urged to share in the patriotic fight to preserve demo-

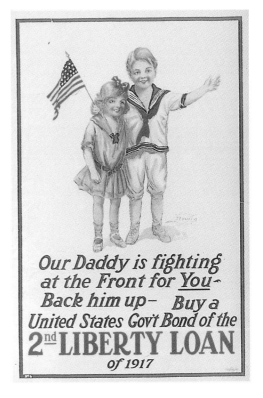

In World War I, as well as in World War II, the bulk of the war expenses was met by borrowing from the public through the sale of government bonds. Posters played an important part in convincing people to buy bonds and help the war effort.

This 1917 poster by an anonymous artist was designed to appeal to recent immigrants to the United States and encourage them to show their loyalty to the country by buying government bonds.

The popular artist Howard Chandler Christy was commissioned to create this poster for the World War I Liberty Loan war bond campaign. The bonds were sold at 3.5 percent interest and raised more than twenty-one billion dollars for the war effort.

cratic principles in the photographic poster series entitled "Produce for Victory," with its appeal primarily to workers, and in the U.S. Crop Corps series, which addressed farmers.

The concept embodied in the famous slogan "Loose Lips Sink Ships" inspired a number of posters that warned against indiscriminate talk that might give military information to an eavesdropping enemy agent; these images were often cartoonlike; but they could also be realistically sentimental, such as one depicting an apprehensive little girl clutching a picture of her soldier-father, underlined by the caption "Don't Kill Her Daddy with Careless Talk."

Similarly, a large part of the propaganda effort demanded sacrifice in terms of daily activities—saving waste fats for use in explosives, saving tin cans, eating leftovers, recycling paper, growing vegetables and canning them, saving gasoline by driving cars slower and fewer miles.

Appeals directly to women became a major element in poster propaganda, from asking women to enlist in the armed forces to encouraging housewives to conserve home resources. Some posters urged women to consider factory work; one example, whose caption reads, "I'm Proud. . .My Husband *Wants* Me to Do My Part," is by artist John Newton Howitt. Photographs of ordinary enlisted men wounded in hospitals, giving such testimony as "She Stood By Me for Hours," adorn posters urging women to join the U.S. Army Nurse Corps. The recruitment posters in general were straightforward. They promoted every branch of the service and were notable for their encouragement of women to become Wacs and Waves and to release men for combat duty.

Of course, there were basic patriotic posters, and some of these ridicule, through repulsive or comic caricatures, the monstrous dictators of the Axis alliance. Cartoon characters were used to promote patriotism—Disney's Donald Duck and Mickey Mouse in the "Appreciate America" series and Al Capp's Li'l Abner and Shmoos to sell U.S. Savings Bonds. The numerous poster ads for bonds in particular sought to evoke a general patriotic response, such as N. C. Wyeth's colorful poster of fighting men, Uncle Sam, war planes, and the American flag, bearing the caption "Buy War Bonds."

But perhaps what made the American posters of World War II stand out from most of their predecessors was the equating of patriotism with democracy. Not merely espousing jingoistic and nationalistic fervor, America's World War II posters rallied the nation's pride by recalling the uniqueness of the country's institutions and its great tradition of freedom and democracy—its flag, its enduring documents, its national monuments, its political heroes, its historic heritage of fighting for liberty. Not only, for example, did the series of posters entitled "This Is America. . .Keep It Free!" spotlight the everyday lives of common people, but it presented America as a country worth fighting for, a land "where you pray to God in your own way," "where public opinion is the basis of national policy," "where a fellow can start on the home team and wind up in the big league," and "where you can dream your dreams and make them come true." In the series depicting national historic sites, "This Is America. . .For This We Fight," the Minuteman statue at Lexington, Massachusetts, reminded us, "Eternal Vigilance Is the Price of Liberty" and the Lincoln Memorial in Washington, D.C., proclaimed, "Government of the People, by the People, for the People Shall Not Perish."

Possibly the most famous of America's wartime posters celebrating the nation's heritage of liberty was the "Four Freedoms" series—four paintings by Norman Rockwell, originally reproduced in the *Saturday Evening Post* and inspired by the theme of President Roosevelt's 1941 state-of-the-union address. They depicted freedom from fear, freedom from want, freedom of speech, and

Posters in both world wars urged people to contribute to the Red Cross. The top poster is by the well-known illustrator and printmaker Gordon Grant. The literal and realistic style of this World War I image contrasts with the simple and more graphic approach of the World War II poster above.

freedom of worship. This timeless series, by one of the nation's finest and most beloved illustrators, perhaps represented the quintessential World War II appeal—the pride in our democratic heritage exemplified through the activities of ordinary Americans.

Indeed, more than propaganda, more than popular art often brilliant in concept and design, America's posters of World War II serve as glowing testimonials to a nation's image of itself as a shining democracy, a land where liberty-loving people of various backgrounds could work together to achieve greatness.

G. H. Gregory

New York
1993

This poster was designed to encourage young men to join the U.S. Navy during World War I. The same painting, by an anonymous artist, was used with different slogans in the navy's recruitment campaign.

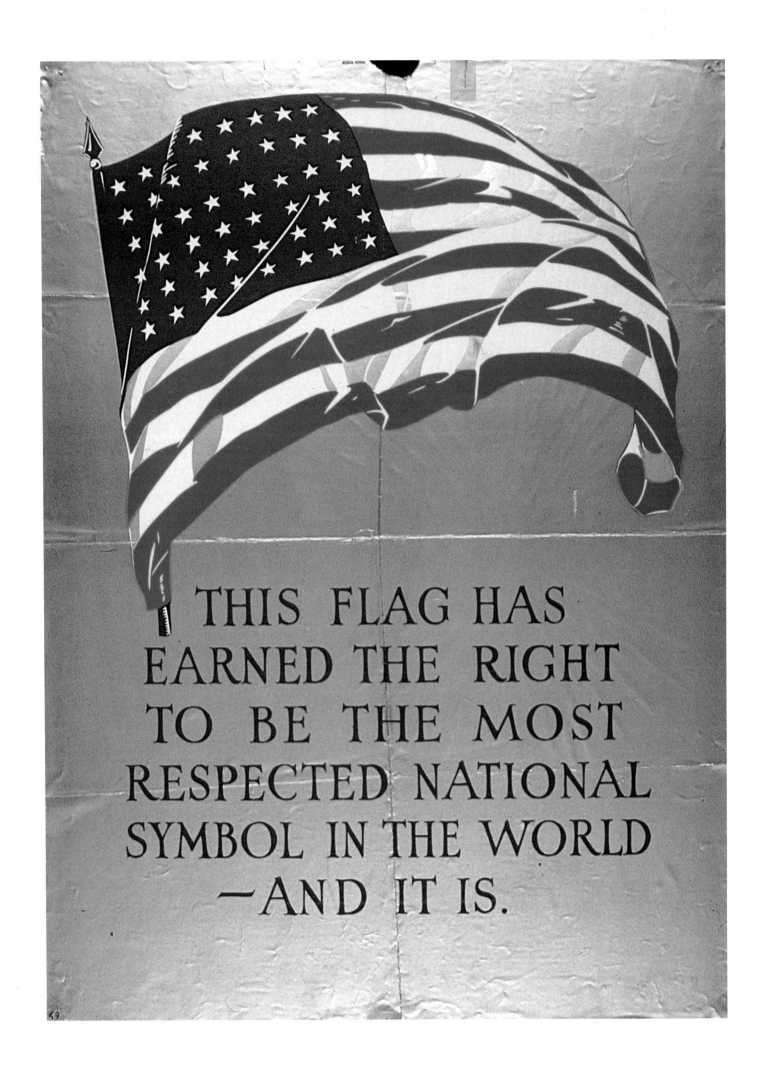

In 1940, Congress authorized the first peacetime conscription in the nation's history. Under the terms of the Selective Training and Service Act, all men between the ages of twenty-one and thirty-five were required to register for possible military service. In response to the army's demand for more manpower, Congress lowered the draft age to eighteen in late 1942. The army recruiting poster left is by Lt. Col. Tom B. Woodburn.

James Montgomery Flagg originally painted the recruiting poster on the right for the U.S. Army in World War I. The image is so strong and so memorable that the poster was revised for use in World War II.

WE CLEAR THE WAY

THE CORPS OF
ENGINEERS
UNITED STATES ARMY

These 1942 recruitment posters for the U.S. Army Signal Corps and the Corps of Engineers were painted by Jes Wilhelm Schlaikjer for the U.S. War Department, Bureau of Public Relations.

Lt. Col. Tom B. Woodburn was commissioned by the U.S. War Department, Bureau of Public Relations, to create this U.S. Army recruitment poster. By the end of the war, in 1945, about five million men had enlisted voluntarily for military service.

Created as the Women's Army Auxiliary Corps (W.A.A.C.) in 1942, the organization was renamed the Women's Army Corps (W.A.C.) in 1943, when it became a regular component of the army. In World War II, approximately one hundred thousand women enlisted to do noncombatant jobs, in the United States and all overseas theaters of operation, to release men for combat duty.

WAAC

DAN V SMITH

THIS IS MY WAR TOO!
WOMEN'S ARMY AUXILIARY CORPS
UNITED · STATES · ARMY

Both of the posters above were designed to encourage enlistment in the U.S. Army Air Force. By the end of the war about three million men served in this branch of the services.

The Department of the Army commissioned Lt. Col. Tom B. Woodburn to create a series of six posters, including this one on the left, which was issued in 1940.

During World War I women were admitted into the navy as "yeomen (F)." In World War II women were permitted to enlist and receive commissions in the Women's Reserve of the U.S. Naval Reserve. They were called Waves, an acronym for Women Accepted for Volunteer Emergency Service. By the end of the war, in 1945, about eighty-six thousand women had enlisted for noncombatant duty.

By the end of the war there were more than four million men serving in the navy, including the submarine service.

He volunteered for
SUBMARINE SERVICE

LET'S GO!

U·S·MARINES

First printed on December 30, 1941, the poster left is one of the first World War II recruitment posters for the U.S. Marine Corps. The artist, known only by the initials T.W.Y., was a U.S. marine.

The poster for the U.S. Marine Corps right is by Haddon H. Sundblom and was issued in 1942. In World War II approximately six hundred seventy-five thousand men enlisted in the marines.

SETTING THE COURSE TO

Victory

WITH THE U.S. COAST GUARD

In wartime the coast guard moves from the Department of the Treasury into the navy. In World War II about two hundred fifty thousand men served in the coast guard.

Nurses were badly needed in the war, in which about six hundred seventy thousand men were wounded in combat.

Nurses Are Needed Now!

"I'D HAVE BEEN A GONER . . ."

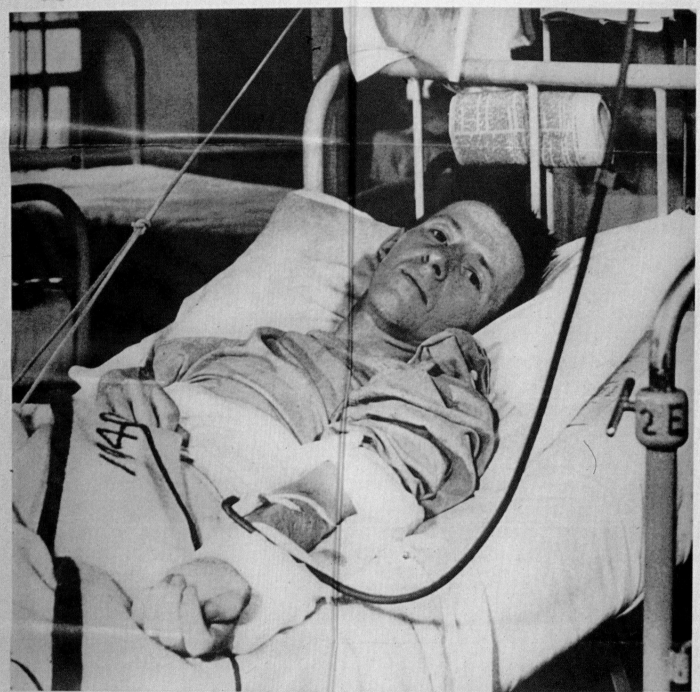

STAFF SERGEANT JOHN SCHUSTER, infantryman from Stelton, New Jersey

"'Hit the ditch, boys; here come the Jerries.' Like the rest of the men I dove for the nearest hedgerow in a Normandy field on the road to St. Lo. The low-flying planes dumped their bombs along the road. Only one missed and that one hit near me. I was badly wounded by the shell fragments and the next thing I knew I was in an evacuation hospital and an Army nurse was giving me blood plasma. If it had'nt been for that I'd have been a goner. I'm an old hand at plasma for I've had it twenty times. Now they're giving me whole-blood transfusions. There were Army nurses with me all the time and, tired as many of them were, they'd spend their off-duty time with us wounded men, helping to bring us back to where we thought things were really worth fighting for. We need all the nurses we can get. If you can, join the Army Nurse Corps."

MORE NURSES ARE NEEDED   U. S. ARMY NURSE CORPS

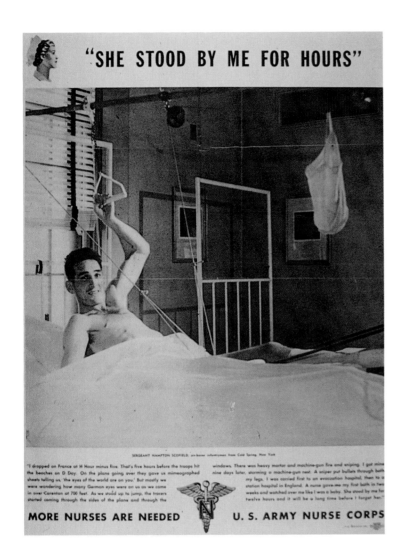

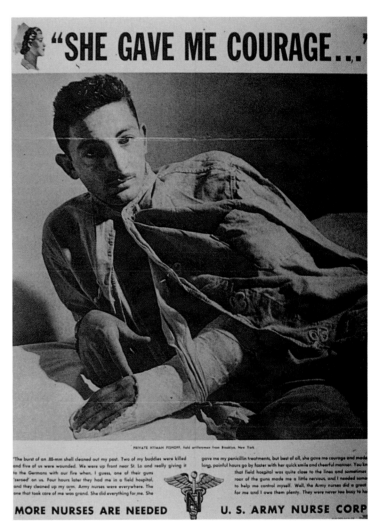

These three recruitment posters for the U.S. Army Nurse Corps feature photographs of wounded soldiers and their moving testimonials.

THIS IS AMERICA
—*for this we fight*

Ohio River Steamboat on One of America's Inland Waterways

May Only Ships of Peace
Be Borne on Our Rivers

This poster, and those in the series shown on the following pages, were displayed in public buildings all over the country.

28

THIS IS AMERICA
—for this we fight

This Stately Elm Has Guarded This American Home for Generations

Bloom Forever, O Republic
As Has This Elm Since Our Nation's Birth

THIS IS AMERICA
—for this we fight

Lighthouse, Montauk Point, N. Y.

May Its Radiance Light Safely
The Way to Ports of Freedom

THIS IS AMERICA
—for this we fight

El Capitan, Yosemite National Park

From Every Mountain-Side
Let Freedom Ring

THIS IS AMERICA
—*for this we fight*

The Minuteman, Lexington, Mass.

Eternal Vigilance Is the Price of Liberty

THIS IS AMERICA
—for this we fight

Mt. Rushmore National Memorial, Honoring Washington, Jefferson, Theodore Roosevelt and Lincoln

Heroes of the Republic—
An Inspiration to the Heroes of Today

THIS IS AMERICA
—for this we fight

The American Family Looks Ahead

UNITED WE STAND

THIS IS AMERICA
—for this we fight

IN THIS TEMPLE
AS IN THE HEARTS OF THE PEOPLE
FOR WHOM HE SAVED THE UNION
THE MEMORY OF ABRAHAM LINCOLN
IS ENSHRINED FOREVER

Lincoln Memorial, Washington, D.C.

Government of the People–by the People
–for the People–Shall Not Perish

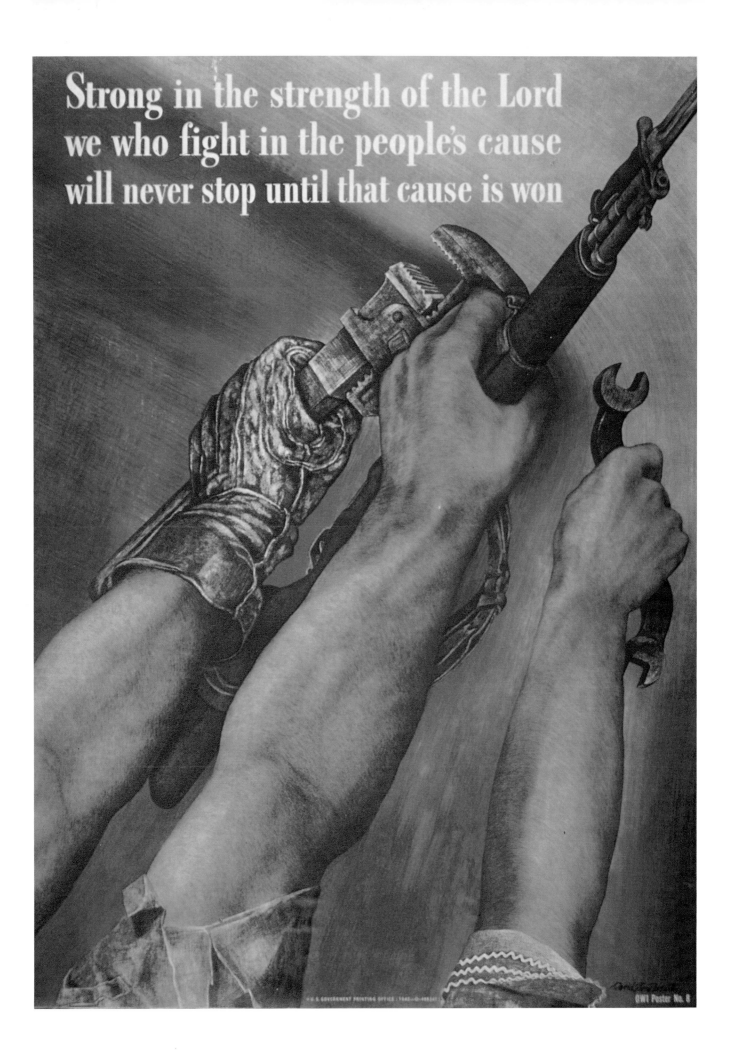

TOGETHER WE WIN

Get behind your labor-management committee

These two posters used similar symbolism to promote cooperation among various segments of American society. The Office of War Information released the poster on the left in 1942. David Stone Martin is the artist.

Walt Disney helped in the war effort on the home front. In the posters above, Donald Duck asks people to support rationing and Mickey Mouse urges them to buy defense bonds and savings stamps.

Despite increased revenue from taxes, during World War II the federal government relied upon borrowing through the sale of war bonds and small-denomination war stamps to meet most of the war costs. By July 1945, the government had conducted seven successful war-bond drives, which had raised a total of almost sixty-one billion dollars.

THIS WORLD CANNOT EXIST HALF SLAVE AND HALF FREE

BUY WAR BONDS

The Canadian poster left was one of many created to draw attention to the Victory Bond campaign as part of the country's war effort. Motion picture shorts featuring film stars were also used as part of the bond campaign.

The poster right served as a thank-you to the newsboys of America for their great contribution to the war effort.

Thanks Buddy!

NEWSPAPER BOYS HAVE SOLD OVER 1¼ BILLION
WAR SAVINGS STAMPS SINCE PEARL HARBOR

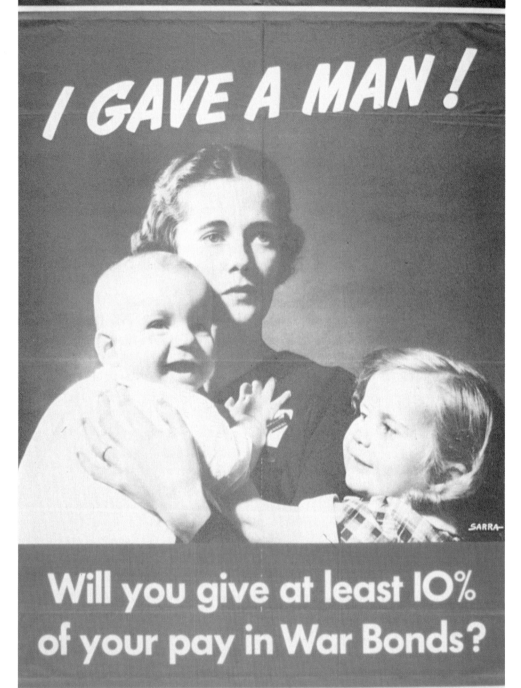

Come On, C-H.... Do More!
This Isn't Peace - IT'S WAR!!

I GAVE A MAN!

Will you give at least 10%
of your pay in War Bonds?

SIGN UP FOR WAR BONDS
Make your department 100%

SARRA

Individual companies used Sarra's basic poster, left, in their war bond drives in factories and offices.

The U.S. Treasury Department released the touching poster on the right in 1943.

Lexington, 1775

They fought for Freedom
We fight to keep it

BUY WAR STAMPS & BONDS

INDEPENDENCE
July 4, 1776

"...and for the support of this declaration, with a firm reliance, on the protection of Divine Providence, we mutually pledge to each other our Lives, our Fortunes and our sacred Ho..."

They kept the faith and so do you every time
you lend a dime for WAR SAVINGS STAMPS

To exhibit these posters to best advantage please cut
apart along the dotted lines and display separately

JOHN PAUL JONES said:

'I have not yet begun to fight'

Fight with War Stamps & Bonds

Washington crossed the Delaware

to win our Freedom
We cross oceans to keep it

BUY WAR STAMPS & BONDS

Four woodcut-style images evoke the spirit of the Revolutionary War patriots in this series of four posters promoting the sale of war stamps and bonds. Published together on one sheet, they were intended to be cut apart and displayed separately.

N. C. Wyeth, the well-known artist, was commissioned by the federal government to do the poster on the right. It was printed by the Government Printing Office in 1942.

44

BUY WAR BONDS

In 1945, the U.S. Treasury commissioned C. C. Beall to create the poster at left to promote the 7th War Loan campaign. It shows U.S. marines raising the flag on Mount Suribachi on Iwo Jima.

The well-known cartoonist Al Capp created the poster right, featuring the Shmoos and Li'l Abner, to encourage people to buy U.S. Savings Bonds.

The tremendous achievement of the United States in World War II of mobilizing the entire country's resources was influenced by the federal government's intensive program of marshaling the contributions of people of all ages and from all walks of life. This is clearly demonstrated in the series of posters that begins on this page.

This is America..

Where a fellow can start on the home team and wind up in the big league. Where there is always room at the top for the fellow who has it on the ball ★ *This is your America!*

...Keep it Free!

49

This is America..

. . . where your little ones of today will be the big people of tomorrow. Where free education prepares them for the full opportunities of democracy ★ *This is your America*

...Keep it Free!

This is America...

...where public opinion is the basis of national policy ... where the voice of the people is the voice that counts ★ This is <u>your</u> America

... Keep it Free!

This is America...

.... where you can have your "say" about anything, without fear or worry. Where freedom of speech is a right nobody can take away from you ★ This is your America

... Keep it Free!

This is America..

.... where you pray to God in your own way, according to your own beliefs, in the peace and blessing of religious tolerance. Where freedom of belief and action has built a great nation ★ *This is your America.*

...Keep it Free!

...Yes, son, this is America, where you can dream your dreams and make them come true. Where freedom to do ... to think ... to speak is your right and your heritage. Protect it forever ★ *This is <u>your</u> America*

During World War II, images of Uncle Sam were used to promote national security, especially in plants that were producing war materials under government contracts. Both these posters were inspired by James Montgomery Flagg's 1917 "I Want You for the U.S. Army" poster.

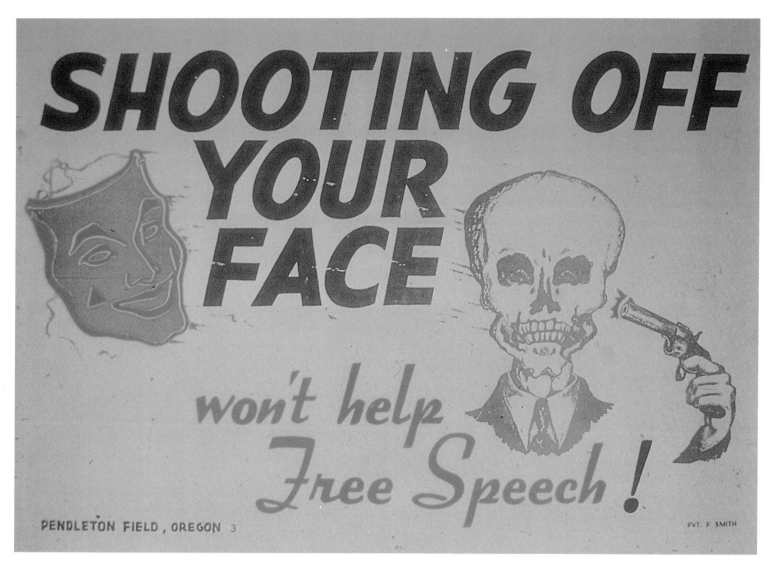

Pvt. F. Smith produced this
crude appeal for discretion
to his fellow rookies at
Pendleton Field, Oregon.

With German and Japanese submarines patroling
off U.S. coasts, great emphasis was placed on
educating servicemen and civilians about the need
for secrecy concerning military matters, especially
troop movements.

★ SILENCE MEANS SECURITY ★

Protect his future
...watch your tongue

★ SILENCE MEANS SECURITY ★

DON'T KILL HER DADDY
WITH CARELESS TALK

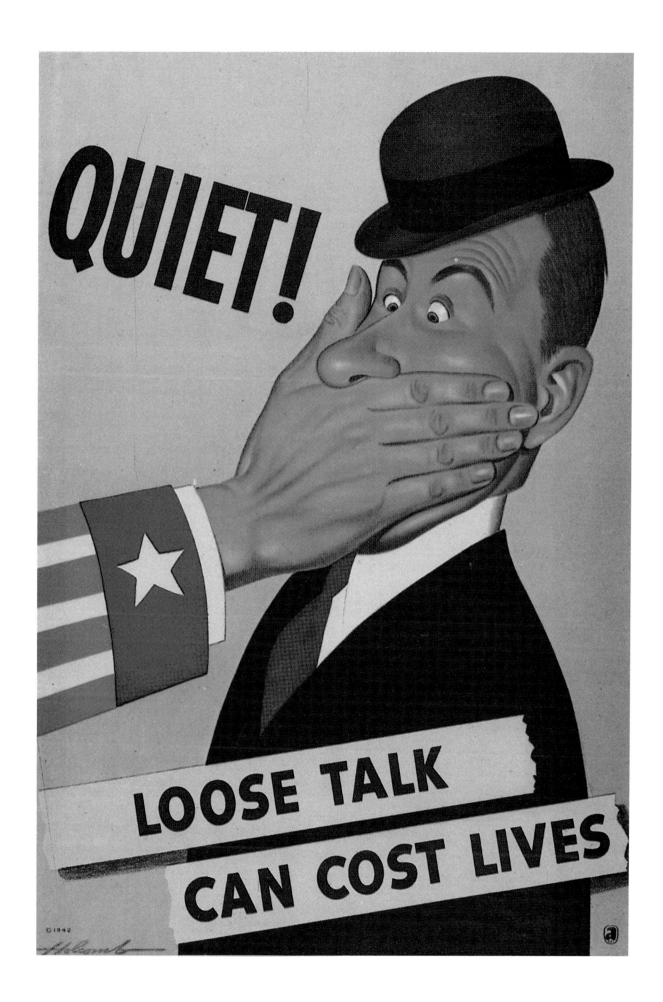

Patriotic posters, which were often humorous, urged Americans to be security conscious.

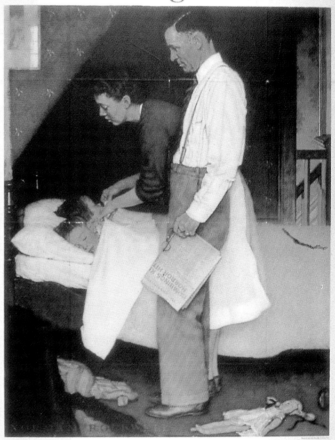

OURS...to fight for

FREEDOM FROM WANT

OURS...to fight for

FREEDOM FROM FEAR

The popular artist Norman Rockwell originally created the paintings of the four freedoms—freedom from fear, freedom from want, freedom of speech, and freedom of worship—for the *Saturday Evening Post*. These now famous, timeless images were released as posters by the Office of War Information in 1943.

The four posters on the following pages combine poetry and bold images in an appeal for support of the nations that were under the yoke of German occupation. The paintings are by the well-known illustrators Everett Henry, Allen Saalburg, Stevan Dohanos, and John Atherton.

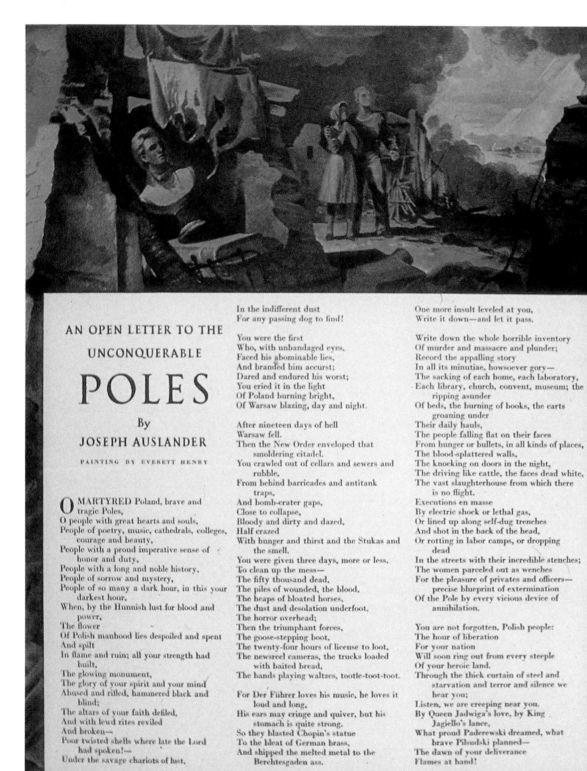

AN OPEN LETTER TO THE

UNCONQUERABLE

POLES

By

JOSEPH AUSLANDER

PAINTING BY EVERETT HENRY

O MARTYRED Poland, brave and
tragic Poles,
O people with great hearts and souls,
People of poetry, music, cathedrals, colleges,
courage and beauty,
People with a proud imperative sense of
honor and duty,
People with a long and noble history,
People of sorrow and mystery,
People of so many a dark hour, in this your
darkest hour,
When, by the Hunnish lust for blood and
power,
The flower
Of Polish manhood lies despoiled and spent
And spilt
In flame and ruin; all your strength had
built,
The glowing monument,
The glory of your spirit and your mind
Abused and rifled, hammered black and
blind;
The altars of your faith defiled,
And with lewd rites reviled
And broken—
Poor twisted shells where late the Lord
had spoken!—
Under the savage chariots of lust.

In the indifferent dust
For any passing dog to find!

You were the first
Who, with unbandaged eyes,
Faced his abominable lies,
And branded him accurst;
Dared and endured his worst;
You cried it in the light
Of Poland burning bright,
Of Warsaw blazing, day and night.

After nineteen days of hell
Warsaw fell.
Then the New Order enveloped that
smoldering citadel.
You crawled out of cellars and sewers and
rubble,
From behind barricades and antitank
traps,
And bomb-crater gaps,
Close to collapse,
Bloody and dirty and dazed,
Half crazed
With hunger and thirst and the Stukas and
the smell.
You were given three days, more or less,
To clean up the mess—
The fifty thousand dead,
The piles of wounded, the blood,
The heaps of bloated horses,
The dust and desolation underfoot,
The horror overhead;
Then the triumphant forces,
The goose-stepping boot,
The twenty-four hours of license to loot,
The newsreel cameras, the trucks loaded
with baited bread,
The bands playing waltzes, tootle-toot-toot.

For Der Führer loves his music, he loves it
loud and long,
His ears may cringe and quiver, but his
stomach is quite strong.
So they blasted Chopin's statue
To the bleat of German brass,
And shipped the melted metal to the
Berchtesgaden ass.

One more insult leveled at you,
Write it down—and let it pass.

Write down the whole horrible inventory
Of murder and massacre and plunder;
Record the appalling story
In all its minutiae, howsoever gory—
The sacking of each home, each laboratory,
Each library, church, convent, museum; the
ripping asunder
Of beds, the burning of books, the carts
groaning under
Their daily hauls,
The people falling flat on their faces
From hunger or bullets, in all kinds of places,
The blood-splattered walls,
The knocking on doors in the night,
The driving like cattle, the faces dead white,
The vast slaughterhouse from which there
is no flight.
Executions en masse
By electric shock or lethal gas,
Or lined up along self-dug trenches
And shot in the back of the head,
Or rotting in labor camps, or dropping
dead
In the streets with their incredible stenches;
The women parceled out as wenches
For the pleasure of privates and officers—
precise blueprint of extermination
Of the Pole by every vicious device of
annihilation.

You are not forgotten, Polish people:
The hour of liberation
For your nation
Will soon ring out from every steeple
Of your heroic land.
Through the thick curtain of steel and
starvation and terror and silence we
hear you;
Listen, we are creeping near you.
By Queen Jadwiga's love, by King
Jagiello's lance,
What proud Paderewski dreamed, what
brave Pilsudski planned—
The dawn of your deliverance
Flames at hand!

AN OPEN LETTER TO THE UNCONQUERABLE

CZECHOSLOVAKS

By JOSEPH AUSLANDER

PAINTING BY ALLEN SAALBURG

THIS is not a letter that starts,
"Dear So-and-So,"
And ends,
"Faithfully yours." Ah, no,
Brave hearts
And gallant friends,
This is a letter that a man
Heavy with words makes;
In my case, an ordinary American,
Whose hand shakes
Because, knowing the tremendous truth,
The words choke up in his mouth.

My mind goes back to Munich,
Goes back to the beginning—
The little Caesar, hand upraised, hand in
      tunic,
Gaping and glaring and grinning
Under his mustache; the cheers,
The "Sieg Heils" dinning
Drunken music in his ears;
My mind goes back
To the cowardly bivouac
Under the umbrella, under

The alpine parasol where you were torn
      asunder
To appease the Nazi appetite for plunder.

You were the blood-bright spur
To prick the languid conscience of this age;
You were the cage
Wherein the Executioner,
That arch-sadist,
Of all mad dogs the maddest,
Might practice the refinements of his rage;
The laboratory, soundproof, leisurely,
      clinical,
Where, quite begloved, bespatted,
      monocled and cynical,
The fiend could vent
In hideous experiment
His hate of God and man, of saint and sage.

Hangmen die too;
Bullets from nowhere through the spine
Make hangmen whine,
Turn hangmen's faces blue;
If they have long enough to remember,
They may recall
The name of one Jan Opletal,
Young medical student at Prague,
His death from wounds in the night,
His funeral,

The seventeenth of November;
The streets churning with Czech and
      Slovak youth; the sudden brawl,
Deliberately provoked; the foremost fall,
Shot down by storm troopers; they lurch,
      they sprawl;
A few crawl
Away to die like any beaten dog.
This is only the curtain raiser; the epilogue
Follows; the student hostels are surrounded,
Boys and girls riddled by Schmeissers,
      tortured, abused, pounded
Into submission; eyes gouged out, earlobes
      torn off, hounded
From horror to horror. . . . Turn your
      face to the wall,
Hangman; death will soon enfold in fog
The sickening sound, the smell, the sight
Of this blood-soaked Walpurgis Night.

But never, hangman, never from your face
Shall death or time or blood erase
That massacre of youth,
Nor any self-dug death pits hide one trace
Of their fierce love of truth;
Break the head
Of every stubborn hostage; shoot him dead
Until the earth runs red;
Others will stand in his stead.
You sow the dragon's tooth.
Burn a hundred Lidices to the ground.
New Lidices will spring up; the desolate space
Charred, choked with ashes,
And dead birds all around
Will consecrate a holy place
Drenched with the blood that flames and
      flashes
Wherever Czechoslovaks and freedom's
      dream are found.

AN OPEN LETTER TO THE UNCONQUERABLE

NORWEGIANS

By JOSEPH AUSLANDER

PAINTING BY STEVAN DOHANOS

I KNOW you, Norway;
Your blood runs bright in my little daughter,
Your beauty runs warm and wild
In my girl child.
You are a queen, standing in a doorway,
Staring out over the long water,
Remembering the ships,
Remembering the boys and girls with
    yellow hair
And the laughter struck dead on their lips.
You are a woman with a beautiful name,
Remembering how the new barbarians came.

I see you as I saw you long ago,
Standing so,
Lingering in the doorway
Of your blue water,
O noble Norway,
Whose blood runs bright in my little daughter.
The evening was warm,
The twilight long,
The summer sun
Fastened gold fingernails to the horizon in a slow
Reluctant afterglow.
That was before the storm,
That was before the blow,
That was before the Hun,
The steel-winged swarm,
Swept the sweet land with flame,
That was before the new barbarians came.

I remember the small farms
That cover the countryside
With harvests of courage and pride,
And the women with open arms
Welcoming the sickly German lad;
Giving the German boys the best they had,
Feeding them at the table with their own
    sons—
These were the same, the very same
Who came back later, who came
With slaughter and flame,
With tanks and guns,
With bayonets and bombs,
To the friendly homes,
To their foster fathers and mothers,
To their foster sisters and brothers,
Speaking the language with all its charms,
Spouting all its graces,
Spitting it into the people's faces.

I see you as I saw you that last long summer
Before the bomber
Let loose hell,
Before the sky fell
In flame.
You are the same proud people, yet not
    the same;
Your eyes are frozen blue steel,
Your mouths are stone,
Your hands hard as bone;

There are faces I do not see, but feel.
Many are gone;
Some dead—never mind how, just dead
For something their hands did, their
    mouths said,
Their eyes read.
Some fled
In little fishing boats, in leaky crates,
By night, on skis, on skates,
To England, to Canada, to the United States;
Some stained the snow, the water, the ground;
Some drowned
And were never found.

They will return,
O Norway, mother of heroes,
Mother of patriots,
Mother of men!
They will come back from everywhere,
By ocean, land and air—
They will come back, and then
There will be shots;
They will burn
The filth of the Nazi Neros;
There will be a tremendous house cleaning.
The sky will be washed free
Of the foulness, the infamy.
Your young eagles will give the sky over
    Norway a new meaning.
Every street, house, factory,
Every farm and field
Will have to be cauterized and healed.
This will take time, beloved land,
But I shall again see you stand
Like a queen called home from heroic exile,
    the church bells ringing,
The people crying and laughing and
    shouting and singing!
You will look out over the long blue water,
The clean light on your hair
As you linger there
In your doorway,
Ah, dear mother of my little daughter!
Norway!

AN OPEN LETTER TO THE

UNCONQUERABLE

DUTCH

By

JOSEPH AUSLANDER

PAINTING BY JOHN ATHERTON

TRAPPED between the devil
And the deep blue sea,
You were laid level
With your long neutrality.
What is good faith good for?
Everything honor and decency stood for;
This is what you spill your blood for;
This is war.
The devil is cunning, the blue sea is deep.
So you slept, warm in your woolly
        innocence, and free;
So you slumbered,
Not dreaming your days of liberty were
        numbered.
Ah, sleep no more, Holland, sleep no more;
The Gauleiter of Darkness, the Overlord
        of Evil,
Hitler hath murdered sleep.

How merrily did the Master Race measure
Along the cloudless heaven at their leisure
The massacre of Rotterdam.
Opening their bomb bays, oh, so slowly,
Tasting the fine deliberate pleasure
Like something holy,
As one might sow an acre freshly plowed,
So they sowed flame and death into the crowd.

A century
Of peace in five spring days
Perished among the tulips in full blaze,
Sprawled dead among the hyacinths
        whose sweet smell
Heralded this last loveliest of Mays
And hell
As well.
There are offenses so foul,
So rank
In the black chronicle of crime,
They give the soul
So huge a wrench
As leaves an everlasting stench
In the nostrils of time;
So the Rotterdam horror stank.
Even the murky aboriginal demon
At ambush in the breast of slave and
        freeman
Shrinks from it,
And conscience itself recoils and sickens
        in one enormous vomit.

Before their honest and bewildered eyes,
Men dropping from the skies
In Dutch disguise—
Behold, the apostles of the new heroic
        morality
Of treachery
And lechery
And lies.
"We do not come as enemies,"
They blandly said,
And put a bullet through the farmer's
        head
And left him dead
In his own tulip bed;
The cattle graze
In the green meadows.
They gaze
At the ballooning shadows
That sway and fall and rise and run
        together
And fill this quiet weather
At a breath
With shots, confusion, terror, blood and
        death.

Policemen, firemen, letter carriers, grocers,
        nuns
Bristling suddenly with hand grenades and
        guns.
That amiable next-door neighbor,
The pastry cook's continually smiling lodger
Whose lip curled livid with an old slash of
        the saber—
Funny codger—
The bicycle-shop keeper, so droll and
        solemn,
Whose pockets were always bulging with
        odds and ends—
All these good neighbors, good friends—
The Fifth Column!

Five days and nights of tumult, lewd and
        vague
And monstrous like some vile nightmarish
        mist
Swarmed over The Hague,
The plague
Enveloped the Moerdijk Bridge as with a
        slippery fist.
Forget nothing; warm your hearts with
        the heroic list:
Remember Waalhaven and the sailors
        fallen
With that good gallant vessel, the Van
        Galen.
Remember, through proud tears,
The battle of Kornwerderzand;
The brave little band
Of Grenadiers
Storming the airdromes, again and again,
        re-forming
Their shattered lines for still another
        storming.
Remember, all the days of your years,
That when the world stood tottering and
        shaken,
The dike of the Zuider Zee was never
        taken.
Remember the night
Of Venlo and the dynamite. . . .
Remember . . . forget nothing . . . fight . . .
        fight . . . fight. . . .

GIVE IT YOUR BEST!

Commissioned by the
Office of Emergency
Management in 1942, the
poster above, by Charles
Coiner, was intended to
boast war production.

The drawing on the right was used for various
posters in several countries, including the United
States. It was done by Käthe Kollwitz, the famous
German artist whose powerful graphics condemned
hunger, distress, war, and fascism.

Ask the women and children whom Hitler is starving whether rationing is too great a "sacrifice"

Housewives and butchers all over the country were mobilized to collect cooking fats for conversion to explosive ingredients.

FATS HELP MAKE GUNPOWDER
a tablespoon each day from your kitchen
will crush the Axis

MOVIE STAR JANET BLAIR LADLES EXTRA FAT FROM THE ROASTING PAN. While edible fats should give all possible nutrition before going to war, some can be taken from the pan before making gravy. To meet war needs, every housewife must save one tablespoonful of fat each day.

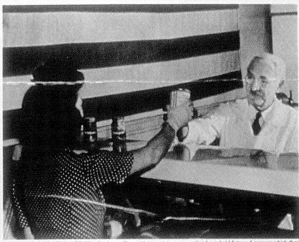

TAKE THE FAT TO YOUR BUTCHER. Butchers all over the country are accepting household fats and greases which they will turn over to local rendering plants for conversion into glycerine. They will pay you for each pound of fat the price established by the official collection agency.

THE SOAP MAKER EXTRACTS THE GLYCERINE. Glycerine results from a soap making process. Glycerine makes explosives and camouflage paints. In this giant soap kettle fats become soap. When salt is added, the liquid part of this mixture will drop to the bottom of the kettle. That liquid, in the hands of chemists, becomes glycerine.

ACIDS TRANSFORM GLYCERINE INTO NITROGLYCERINE. When nitric and sulphuric acids are added to glycerine it becomes deadly nitroglycerine for explosives. When glycerine is allocated to one of our allies, it is usually shipped in its harmless state.

WASTE FATS HELP CAUSE THIS EXPLOSION. This demolition charge would have blown out a section of railroad track if it had been set under the rails instead of in a bank of earth during maneuvers. A Marine demolition squad in training at the New River, N. C. base goes through the full routine of destroying a strategic railway line.

DEAD ANIMAL FATS ARE USEFUL
Renderers in the rural areas are prepared to process fats from dead farm animals. Your government needs this fat. You are urged to contact your nearest renderer to remove dead animals.

WHERE FAT GOES
One pound of waste fats equals 1/10 of a pound of glycerine. 1/10 of a pound of glycerine equals 1/5 of a pound of nitroglycerine. 1/5 of a pound of nitro-glycerine equals 1.3 pounds of gunpowder. 1/5 of a pound of nitro-glycerine equals 1/2 of a pound of dynamite. 50 pounds of waste cooking fats equals 5 pounds of glycerine, or enough to manufacture synthetic resin sufficient to produce enough camouflage to cover one medium tank.

There was an organized drive to recover all forms of scrap metal for military matériel.

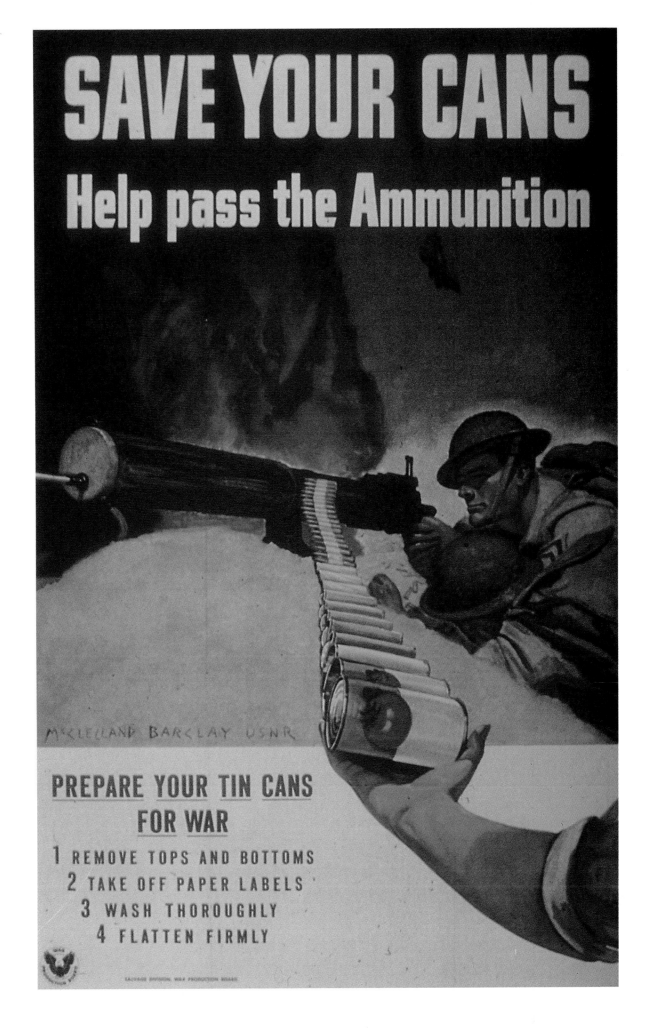

SAVE YOUR CANS
Help pass the Ammunition

PREPARE YOUR TIN CANS FOR WAR

1 REMOVE TOPS AND BOTTOMS
2 TAKE OFF PAPER LABELS
3 WASH THOROUGHLY
4 FLATTEN FIRMLY

Paralleling the federal government's promotion of increased
production of food was the program to curtail its waste.

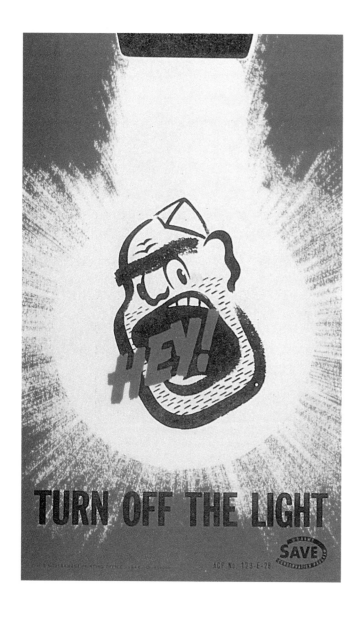

Electricity, silk, paper—only a few of the commodities civilians were urged to conserve for the war effort.

Even Smokey was drafted in support of the conservation of the nation's forests in wartime. These posters were commissioned by the Forest Service of the U.S. Department of Agriculture.

Posters such as these urged American housewives to be productive and thrifty.

The good health of civilians was crucial to war production. Posters like these were displayed in factories and offices.

JUST BY
Keeping Well
YOU can help WIN THIS WAR

With nearly one-third of America's physicians in the armed forces, we must save our remaining doctors' time for serious and unavoidable sickness and accidents.

FOLLOW THESE 5 SIMPLE HEALTH RULES

1. EAT RIGHT

These are the key foods: milk, butter, eggs, fish, meat, cheese, beans and peas, fruit, green leafy vegetables and the yellow ones, whole grain or enriched cereals and bread. Eat 3 good meals a day!

2. GET YOUR REST

Regularity counts most. You can't catch up on lost sleep or missed relaxation! Try to keep on a regular schedule every day. Take it easy for a little while after lunch and dinner. Go to bed on time, get up on time.

3. SEE YOUR DOCTOR ONCE A YEAR

You have your car checked and serviced every thousand miles. Do as much for your body. Physicians can prevent many diseases and illnesses for both children and grownups nowadays. Give your doctor a chance now, BEFORE you get sick. Go to see *him!*

4. KEEP CLEAN

Plenty of baths, lots of soap. Clean hands, clothes, houses, beds! Get fresh air, sunshine. Drink plenty of water.

5. "PLAY" SOME EACH DAY

Romp with the family, visit with friends, take walks, play games—or do whatever you like to give your mind and body a rest from the daily grind on the job. "All work and no play makes Jack a dull boy."

I'll carry mine too!

TRUCKS AND TIRES MUST LAST TILL VICTORY

SARRA

The Office of War Information issued the poster left. The artist is Sarra.

The poster on the right, released by the temporarily established Office of Defense Transportation, reminded civilians that railroads were needed to move troops. During World War II the railroads carried unprecedented numbers of troops and amounts of arms and equipment.

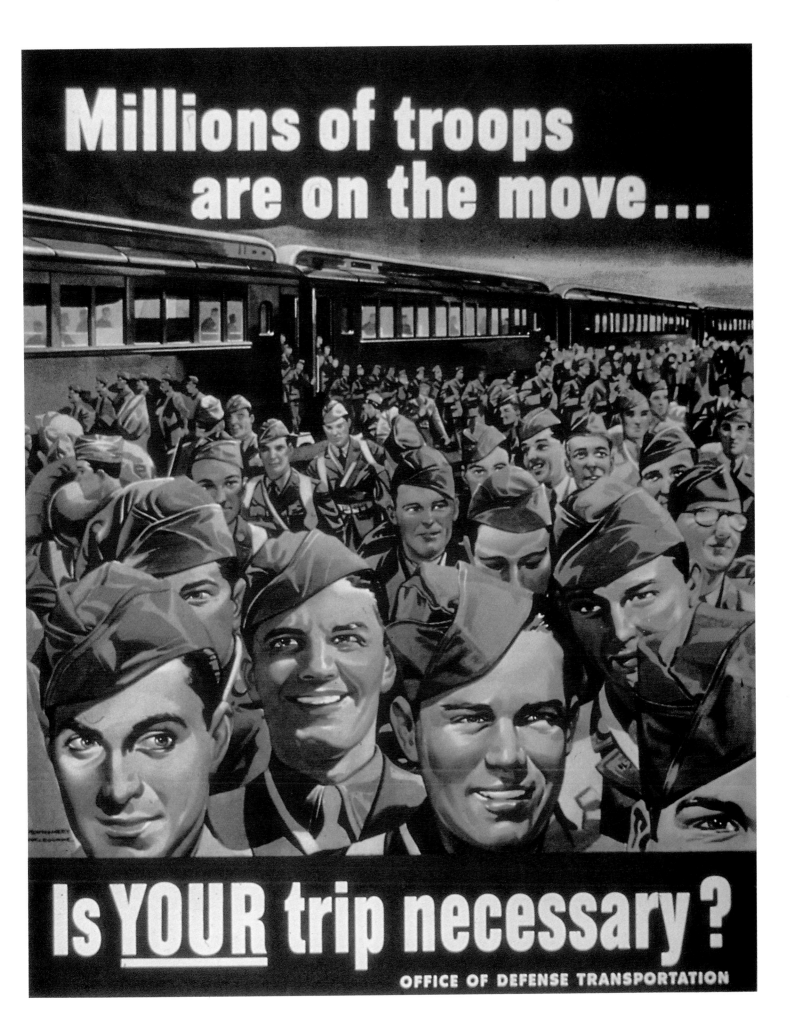

The Office of Price Administration (OPA) fixed prices and rationed such scarce commodities as tires and gasoline.

Educational posters appealed to newly recruited civilians to care for clothes, equipment, and personal health.

For their sake...

AVOID VENEREAL DISEASE

The Office of War Information issued this poster by Allen Saalburg in 1942, a few months after the Japanese attack on Pearl Harbor in Hawaii.

GET A WAR JOB
to help him fight
SEE NEAREST U.S. EMPLOYMENT SERVICE

As a result of the nation's wartime production efforts, there was a critical need for labor. Consequently, women were hired in such numbers that their participation in the job market increased enormously. During the war the employment of women rose from about twelve million to more than eighteen million. By the end of the war women made up about 35 percent of the labor force.

I'm Proud... my husband wants me to do my part

SEE YOUR U. S. EMPLOYMENT SERVICE

WAR MANPOWER COMMISSION

The amusing poster on the left was commissioned by the Texaco Oil Company.

James Montgomery Flagg's rendition of Uncle Sam, right, was utilized to encourage workers on the home front.

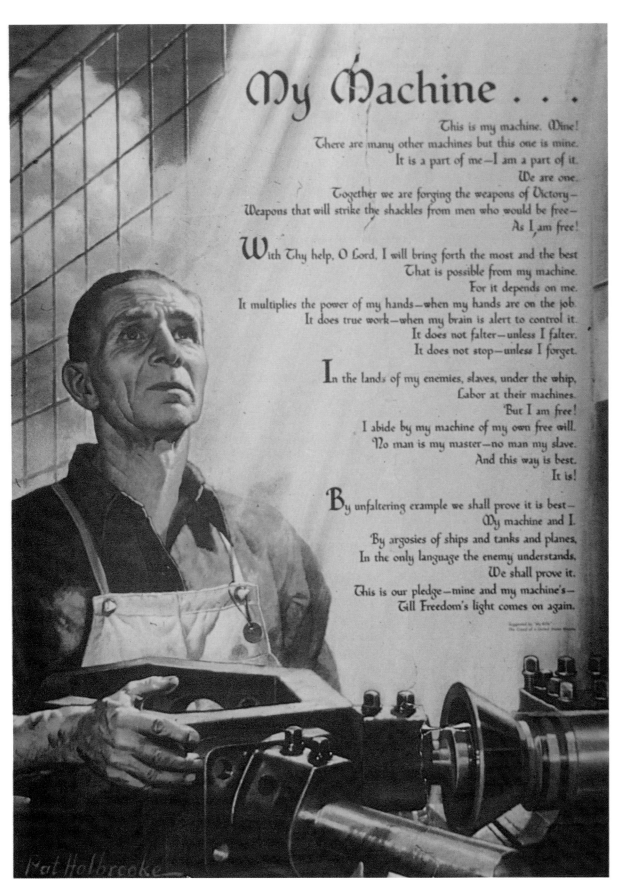

My Machine . . . .

This is my machine. Mine!
There are many other machines but this one is mine.
It is a part of me—I am a part of it.
We are one.
Together we are forging the weapons of Victory—
Weapons that will strike the shackles from men who would be free—
As I am free!

With Thy help, O Lord, I will bring forth the most and the best
That is possible from my machine.
For it depends on me.
It multiplies the power of my hands—when my hands are on the job.
It does true work—when my brain is alert to control it.
It does not falter—unless I falter.
It does not stop—unless I forget.

In the lands of my enemies, slaves, under the whip,
Labor at their machines.
But I am free!
I abide by my machine of my own free will.
No man is my master—no man my slave.
And this way is best.
It is!

By unfaltering example we shall prove it is best—
My machine and I.
By argosies of ships and tanks and planes,
In the only language the enemy understands,
We shall prove it.
This is our pledge—mine and my machine's—
Till Freedom's light comes on again.

Pat Holbrooke

Pat Holbrooke painted this image of a noble worker. It is accompanied by a poem that reveals the man's thoughts—his pride in his role as a machinist who helps make the weapons used in the battle for freedom.

The hero of the Pacific was used in such posters as the one on the right, to inspire civilians to stay on the job.

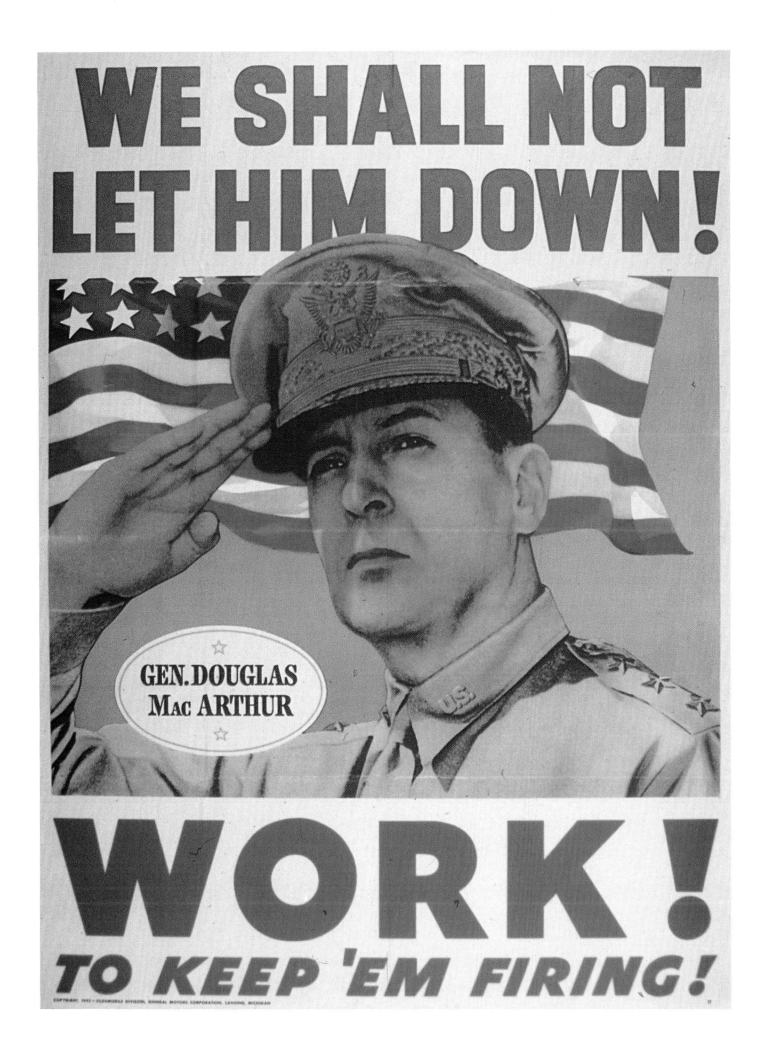

MINE AMERICA'S COAL

"...we'll make it hot for the enemy!"

norman rockwell

SEE YOUR UNITED STATES EMPLOYMENT SERVICE

WAR MANPOWER COMMISSION

Norman Rockwell was commissioned to do the poster left, which was aimed at increasing the production of coal.

Albert Dorne, the famous illustrator, was commissioned by the Armed Service Forces Depots to do the poster right, which was an appeal for efficient production and transportation of supplies.

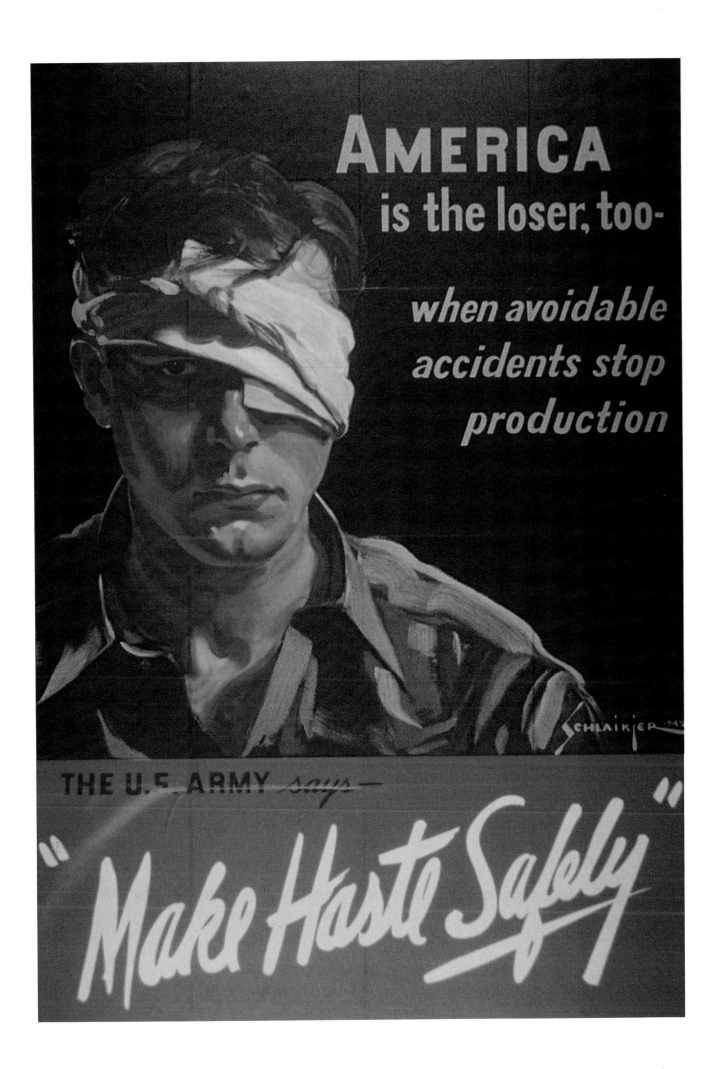

Workers in companies across the country created their own appeals for the war effort.

It was increasingly difficult for farmers to meet the extraordinary demand for foodstuffs. Handicapped by a dwindling work force—many farm workers had joined the armed services or gone to work in factories— farmers looked to the newly established U.S. Crop Corps for much needed help.

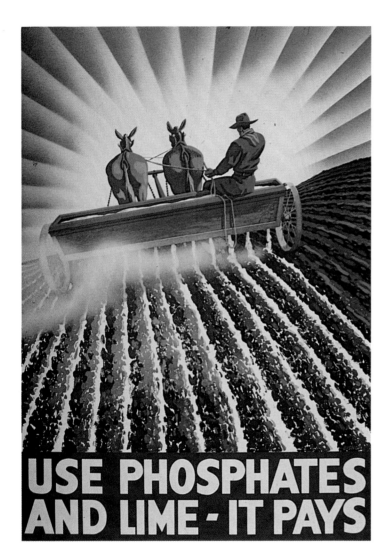

Despite shortages of new agricultural machinery and parts to repair old equipment, America's farmers grew bumper crops. The production and distribution of food was under the supervision of the Food Administration, whose members were appointed by the president.

Jerome Rozen was commissioned in 1944 to do the poster right for the U.S. Commerce Department, Bureau of the Census.

This poster and the fourteen that follow were part of the War Production Board's mobilization of the American peacetime industrial establishment into the mightiest wartime arsenal the world has ever seen. The nine-member board supervised the construction of many new plants and the conversion of existing plants to wartime production. Within one year after the Pearl Harbor attack, the country had manufactured more than forty-seven billion dollars' worth of war matériel, including thirty-two thousand tanks, forty-nine thousand planes, and eight million tons of merchant ships. By the war's end a total of eighty-five thousand tanks, two hundred ninety-five thousand planes, seventy thousand warships, and fifty-five hundred merchant vessels had been produced.

"Full speed ahead! Every moment counts. Time out helps the enemy. That's why we're drivin' hard every minute . . . . . . C'mon, fella, let's step on it."

PRODUCE FOR VICTORY!

"Our Bill of Rights says we are free *men*. Our guns, tanks, planes and ships say...we're going to remain *free men!*"

PRODUCE FOR VICTORY!

"Gosh! Look at 'em fly! My Pop helps make those planes. With flyers like that and workers like my Pop...us Americans are sure gonna win this scrap!"

PRODUCE FOR VICTORY!

"...and God bless daddy and all the American workers who are doing so much to protect freedom and make this a better world for us to live in."

PRODUCE FOR VICTORY!

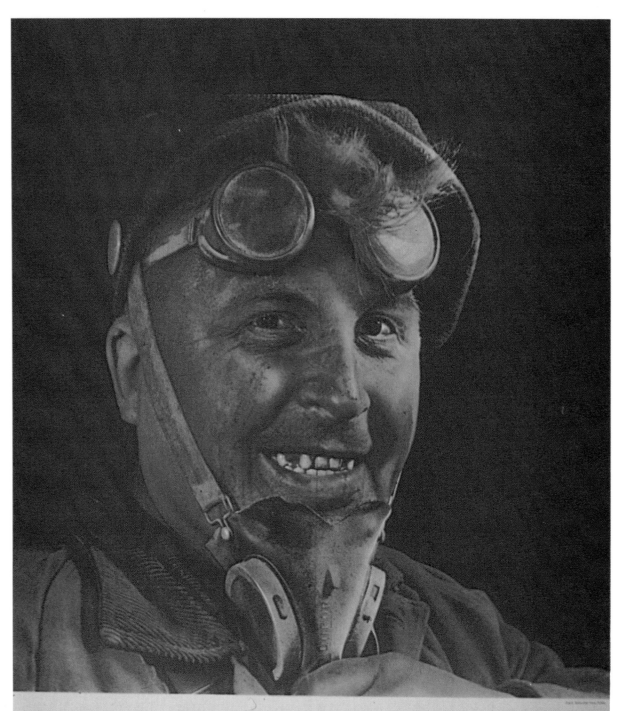

"We're doing it! We're showing the whole cockeyed world what it means when America rolls up its sleeves and goes to work!"

PRODUCE FOR VICTORY!

"America is great because liberty-loving Americans have made it great. You've got to <u>want</u> <u>freedom</u> to work for it — to fight for it — to die for it."

PRODUCE FOR VICTORY!

"Every rivet we drive — every bolt we turn — every ounce we sweat, brings victory a little closer. Breaking production records is the American way of doing things!"

PRODUCE FOR VICTORY!

"*WE*, the Americans of today, know our duty to the Americans of yesterday and the Americans of tomorrow. *WE* shall keep the fires of freedom burning."

PRODUCE FOR VICTORY!

"Man for man, America's workers and America's soldiers are the best in the world! We helped them build our nation . . . we'll help them defend it."

PRODUCE FOR VICTORY!

"This is everybody's war. The enemy has made it so. May you never know what it means to be a refugee ... to be hungry ... to be homeless. *Be sure this never happens to you!*"

PRODUCE FOR VICTORY!

"The stuff our soldiers need is comin'. . . *but fast!* We're workin' like *hell* to give them everything they need to beat the livin' daylights out of those ____!"

PRODUCE FOR VICTORY!

"Thanks America! We British held 'em off for a solid year. Now, together we'll blast the 'blighters' to pulp!"

PRODUCE FOR VICTORY!

"Yesterday, I was a free French worker. Today, I am the slave of the invader. Believe, mon Americain, nothing is important but to keep your freedom—to produce, to build tanks, planes, guns. Destroy the enemy who would take your freedom. For your sake—for God's sake—

PRODUCE FOR VICTORY!

"For more than five years, we, the Chinese, have been fighting with our bare hands. Now, with your planes, tanks and guns... together, we'll give the Japs everything they have coming!"

PRODUCE FOR VICTORY!

"Long may it wave"

Flag-day June 14th 1943

The National Cash Register Company
DAYTON · OHIO